Original Title: 101 STRANGE BUT TRUE SKATEBOARDING FACTS

©101 STRANGE BUT TRUE SKATEBOARDING FACTS, Carlos Martínez Cerdá and Victor Martínez Cerdá, 2023

Authors: Victor Martínez Cerdá and Carlos Martínez Cerdá (V&C Brothers)

© Cover and illustrations: V&C Brothers

Layout and design: V&C Brothers

101
STRANGE BUT TRUE
SKATEBOARDING FACTS

INCREDIBLE AND
SURPRISING EVENTS

1

The GMP Skatepark is currently considered the largest skatepark in the world.

It is located in the city of Guangzhou, China and was built by the company GMP, hence its name.

It has a total area of 16,900 square meters.

This skatepark is known for its wide variety of elements and obstacles for skaters, including a large bowl, ramps, stairs, and rails.

In addition, it has different areas for the practice of different disciplines such as street, bowl, and vert.

The construction of the GMP Skatepark was commissioned by the sportswear company Vans, which was looking to create a unique and spectacular space for skaters.

The design was led by architect and professional skater Chris Miller, who ensured that innovative and challenging elements were included for the skaters.

Despite the GMP Skatepark being currently the largest skatepark in the world, there are other large and renowned skateparks in different parts of the world, such as the Kona Skatepark in the United States, the Prado Skatepark in Brazil, and the Skatelab in Spain.

2

Rodney Mullen is considered by many as the father of most modern skateboarding tricks.

He was born in Florida, United States in 1966, and started skating at the age of 10.

Mullen was the world champion in freestyle skateboarding for several years, and also had success competing in vert and street.

Throughout his career, Mullen invented many of the tricks that are now considered fundamental in skateboarding, including the kickflip, heelflip, 360 flip, casper flip, and many others.

Additionally, he was one of the first skaters to incorporate flatground into his tricks and develop the street skateboarding style.

Mullen is known for his innovative and creative approach to skateboarding, and his ability to blend elements from different disciplines and styles.

His influence on the world of skateboarding has been enormous, and many skaters around the world have been inspired by his tricks and unique approach.

In addition to his skateboarding career, Mullen has also worked as an engineer and designer, and has been an active advocate for safety and education in skateboarding.

He is considered by many as a living legend of skateboarding, and his impact on the sport is undeniable.

3

Skateboarding has its origins in California, United States, in the late 1940s and early 1950s.

Surfers began practicing in the streets when there were not enough waves in the sea to surf.

By the late 1950s, the first skateboards began to be manufactured by companies like Roller Derby Skate Company and Makaha.

The first boards were made of wood and the wheels were made of metal.

Over time, improvements were made in the materials used, including the adoption of urethane wheels that improved the boards' ability to roll smoothly and allowed for more advanced tricks.

Skateboarding became popular during the 1960s, but faded in popularity during the 1970s.

However, in the 1980s it experienced a resurgence and became an increasingly popular sport worldwide.

Since then, skateboarding has evolved into different branches and styles, including street, vert, bowl, freestyle, and downhill, among others.

Currently, skateboarding is considered an extreme sport and has been part of the Olympic Games since 2020.

4

There are different styles of skateboarding, each with their own characteristics and approaches.

Some of the most popular are:

- **Street:** Street skateboarding is one of the most popular styles. In this style, skaters perform tricks on urban obstacles such as stairs, railings, benches, and walls. This style focuses on creativity and technical ability to perform tricks anywhere in the city.

- **Vert:** performed on ramps with a vertical shape, also known as half-pipes. Skaters perform tricks on the top of the ramp, jumping and spinning in the air.

- **Bowl:** Similar to vert style, bowl skateboarding is performed in a pool or similar bowl-shaped structure. Skaters use the transition of the surface to perform tricks such as spins, inverteds, and grinds.

- **Freestyle:** involves performing free-style tricks without the need for specific obstacles. Skaters use their imagination and skill to perform a variety of tricks and moves on the ground.

- **Downhill:** This style involves descending a hill at high speed on a skateboard designed for downhill. Skaters use helmets and other protective equipment to prevent injuries in case of falls or crashes.

- **Old School:** refers to the practice of skateboarding in its oldest form, using antique boards and design elements. Skaters who practice this style often perform classic and free-style tricks, and may use boards of unusual shapes and sizes.

5

The term "posser" is a word derived from
"poser", which in English means "poseur",
someone who pretends to be something
they're not to impress others.

In the world of skateboarding, a "posser" is
someone who dresses like a skater and tries to
appear knowledgeable about the sport, but
in reality, lacks skills on the skateboard
and isn't really interested in learning.

The term became popular in the 1990s when
skateboarding became a cultural trend and
many young people began adopting the skate
aesthetic without actually having
an interest in the sport.

Since then, the word has been used in other
contexts to refer to people who pretend to
be something they're not.

6

Kyle Wester is a professional skater from Colorado who set the world speed record on a skateboard in August 2017.

The feat took place on a closed road in Colorado known as the "Hill of Death".

Wester used a modified skateboard with larger wheels, wider trucks, and a special braking system to keep his speed under control.

The speed achieved by Wester was 89.41 miles per hour (approximately 144 km/h), surpassing the previous record of 81.17 mph (approximately 130 km/h) set by Mischo Erban in 2012.

The feat was confirmed by Guinness World Records judges and was hailed by the skateboarding community as an impressive achievement in the sport's history.

7

ABEC is an acronym that stands for "Annular Bearing Engineering Committee", a committee that established a manufacturing tolerance rating system for bearings in the 1950s.

The ABEC rating system ranges from ABEC-1 to ABEC-9, with ABEC-9 being the highest precision bearing.

Each ABEC level refers to a manufacturing tolerance rating in terms of the precision of the balls, inner ring, and outer ring of the bearing.

However, it's important to note that the ABEC rating doesn't measure the overall quality of a bearing, but rather its precision in manufacturing.

Regarding bearings for skateboarding, an ABEC-7 rating or higher is considered high quality and provides good performance in most situations.

However, many professional skaters prefer bearings with ABEC-9 ratings or higher to achieve the best performance in competitions or high-level tricks.

8

Skateboarding at Tokyo 2020 was one of the most anticipated sports at the Olympic Games.

It was the first time skateboarding was included in the Olympic program as an official sport, and two events were held in the competition: street and park.

In the street event, competitors skated on a course that simulated an urban environment, with stairs, handrails, and curbs, while in the park event, skaters competed on a skatepark specifically designed for the event, with smooth curves and transitions.

The skateboarding competition at the Tokyo 2020 Olympics was very exciting and highlighted by the high quality of the participating skaters.

In total, 12 medals were awarded in the two categories, both for men and women.

Japan dominated the skateboarding event at Tokyo 2020, as they won a total of five medals in the two categories, three gold, one silver, and one bronze.

It was a great victory for Japan, as the host country was able to showcase their skill and passion for the sport.

Brazil also had a good performance in the skateboarding competition, winning three silver medals, while Australia won one gold medal.

Skaters from other countries, such as the United States and France, also had standout performances in the event.

Overall, skateboarding at Tokyo 2020 was a great experience for both athletes and spectators and demonstrated that skateboarding is an exciting and energetic sport that deserves recognition and value at the Olympic level.

9

Tony Hawk is a professional American skateboarder, considered a legend in the world of skateboarding.

He was born on May 12, 1968 in San Diego, California.

He started skating at the age of nine and quickly showed great talent and passion for the sport.

At 14 years old, Tony was already competing at a professional level and won his first world championship in 1983.

Since then, he has won numerous titles and medals in skateboarding competitions, including several world championships.

Tony is also known for having developed and popularized many skateboarding tricks, including the famous "900," a two and a half turn spin in the air on a vertical ramp.

This trick was considered impossible until Tony first performed it in 1999.

In addition to his career as a skateboarder, Tony is an entrepreneur and has created a line of skateboarding video games called "Tony Hawk's Pro Skater."

He has also been the subject of several documentaries and movies related to skateboarding.

Tony Hawk has been an ambassador and promoter of skateboarding for decades, and has helped popularize the sport around the world.

His legacy in the world of skateboarding is enormous, and he is considered by many to be one of the greatest skateboarders of all time.

10

The "Randy 720" was the first footwear designed specifically for skateboarding, and featured a flat sole that provided greater stability and grip on the board.

Although it was not a commercial success, it laid the foundation for the design of skate shoes that would come later.

Vans was one of the companies that took note of the Randy 720 design and improved upon it, creating the first skate shoe model of their brand in 1976, known as the "Vans #95" or "Era."

This model became a classic and is still being produced today.

Since then, numerous footwear brands have created their own skate shoes, adapting to the needs of skaters in terms of durability, grip, and comfort.

Additionally, many skaters have become ambassadors for these brands, collaborating on the design and promotion of new lines of footwear.

11

**A skateboard consists of three basic parts that work together
to allow the skater to move and perform tricks:
the deck, the trucks, and the wheels.**

The deck is the largest and most visible part of the skateboard,
usually made of pressed maple wood.

The top surface of the deck is covered with a layer of abrasive
material, known as grip tape, which provides a firm grip for the
skater and prevents their feet from slipping while performing tricks.

The trucks are the metal pieces that are attached
to the bottom of the deck and hold the wheels.

The trucks consist of a main axle with two small movable pieces
called bushings, which allow the skateboard to
turn in different directions.

They also have a kingpin or pivot, which allows the skateboard
to turn in the desired direction.

The wheels are the part that allows the skateboard to move.

They are generally made of polyurethane and come in
different sizes and hardnesses.

Harder wheels are better for smooth surfaces and allow for greater
speed, while softer wheels are better for rough surfaces
and allow for greater traction.

Finally, bearings are small metal pieces that fit inside the
wheels to allow for smooth and frictionless movement.

Bearings are a crucial part of the skateboard, as they allow the
skater to reach higher speeds and perform smoother tricks.

12

Many skaters can consider themselves ambidextrous in terms of their ability to skate and perform tricks on both feet.

This is because, in skateboarding, most tricks require the use of both feet in a balanced way, which causes skaters to develop skills on both feet over time.

In fact, many skaters regularly practice skating in both regular and goofy stances, which means they have the same level of skill skating with their front foot in either the regular or goofy position.

This is because tricks and lines may require skaters to quickly switch directions and they need to feel comfortable skating in both stances.

Additionally, some skaters also prefer to have a "switch" skating stance, in which they skate with their non-dominant foot in front.

This allows them to perform tricks in an uncommon and sometimes more difficult position, which can surprise other skaters and add more variety to their style.

13

In skateboarding, there are two basic stances: regular stance and goofy stance, which are defined by the placement of the skater's front foot.

Regular stance is when the left foot is in front of the board and the right foot is in the back, while goofy stance is when the right foot is in front of the board and the left foot is in the back.

The choice of stance depends on each skater's personal preference.

Some skaters feel more comfortable in regular stance, while others prefer goofy stance.

Generally, most skaters have a dominant stance, but they can also practice and feel comfortable in the other stance.

It is important to note that the placement of the skater's feet also affects the way tricks are performed, especially tricks that require a turn or rotation in the air.

For example, a trick performed in regular stance may be different from the same trick performed in goofy stance.

14

Goofy stance in skateboarding has become popular and refers to the stance where the skater's right foot is in front of the board.

As for its origin, there are several theories and speculations about how the term emerged.

One of the most common theories is that goofy stance was named after a Disney character called Goofy.

In a 1937 animated short film called "Hawaiian Holiday," Goofy rides a surfboard in the same position now known as goofy stance in skateboarding.

Although this theory is widely spread, there is no solid evidence to support its validity.

Another theory is that the term "goofy" was simply used because it was an easy way to differentiate the skater's right foot position from the more common left foot position in the front.

In other words, the term was used as a practical way to describe the skater's foot position.

In any case, goofy stance is common in skateboarding and has been adopted by many skaters, regardless of its origin.

Ultimately, the most important thing is the skater's skill and not the stance they adopt on the board.

15

In the 1990s, the United States Marine Corps Combat Lab considered the possibility of using skateboards in military operations.

The idea was that soldiers could move more quickly and efficiently in urban areas and urbanized terrain using skateboards.

The United States Marine Corps Combat Lab developed a prototype skateboard that included specific features for military use, such as larger and more durable wheels, metal trucks, and a platform that allowed for the attachment of a soldier's equipment and weapons.

The prototype also included a braking system and a strap to secure the board to the soldier's body during use.

However, the idea of using skateboards in military operations was ultimately discarded due to safety concerns.

There was a fear that soldiers could fall off the boards and suffer injuries, or that skateboards could interfere with other equipment and weapons used in military operations.

Although the use of skateboards in the United States military did not materialize, the prototype developed by the United States Marine Corps Combat Lab has been exhibited on several occasions and is considered an interesting example of how ideas from popular culture can inspire military innovation.

16

The "ollie" is considered one of the most basic and fundamental tricks in skateboarding.

It was invented in the 1970s by skater Alan "Ollie" Gelfand, hence its name.

The "ollie" is performed in two parts: in the first part, the skater stomps hard on the tail of the board to make it bounce on the ground, while simultaneously jumping with both feet.

In the second part, the skater drags their front foot up and forward, causing the board to rise into the air.

Once the board is in the air, the skater must straighten their legs and feet to keep it level, and then land back on it with both wheels at the same time.

The "ollie" is the foundation for many other advanced tricks in skateboarding, such as the "kickflip," "heelflip," "nollie," "fakie ollie," "switch ollie," among others.

Mastering the "ollie" requires practice and patience, but it is a crucial skill that every skateboarder must learn in order to progress in this sport.

17

**Wrists are one of the body parts that suffer
the most injuries in skateboarding.**

This is largely due to falls and the way skateboarders
tend to land on their hands and
wrists when losing balance.

In addition, wrists are subject to a great deal of force and
pressure when used for braking or turning the board,
which can lead to overuse injuries or repetitive strain.

In the United States, for example, it is estimated that
around 65,000 people are treated in hospitals for
skateboarding-related injuries each year.

This is due to a combination of factors, such as the high-
impact nature of the sport, the lack of proper protective
equipment, and the inexperience or lack
of skill of some skateboarders.

It is important for skateboarders to use appropriate
protective gear, such as helmets, wrist guards,
elbow pads, and knee pads, to reduce the risk
of serious injuries.

It is also important for skateboarders to be aware of their
limits and take the time necessary to learn
skills and techniques safely and gradually.

18

The skateboarding industry in the United States has experienced significant growth in recent years thanks to a series of factors.

One of the main factors has been the increased popularity of skateboarding on social media and in the media, which has led to greater attention and exposure for the sport.

Another important factor has been the development of high-level skateboarding competitions, such as the X-Games and Street League, which have attracted skateboarders and fans from around the world and helped elevate the sport's profile globally.

These factors have contributed to an increase in demand for skateboarding equipment and accessories, as well as an increase in the sport's overall popularity.

In 2018, it was estimated that the skateboarding industry in the United States was valued at around $1.9 billion, with an expected annual growth of 3.2% in the coming years.

In addition, the skateboarding industry has also had a significant impact on youth culture and fashion, with skateboarding clothing and accessory brands becoming leading brands in urban fashion.

Overall, the skateboarding industry in the United States has experienced significant growth in recent years, driven by a combination of factors, including media exposure, high-level skateboarding competitions, and the growing popularity of the sport in general.

19

Skateboarding is undoubtedly one of the most popular and practiced activities in the world.

It has become a very popular sport, especially among Generation Z, but also among people of all ages.

Currently, there are over 85 million skaters worldwide and the number continues to grow year after year.

In addition to being a fun and exciting activity, skateboarding has also become a lifestyle and a form of artistic and cultural expression for many young people.

Skaters are often creative and rebellious, and are often associated with music, urban art, and street fashion.

20

At the Tokyo 2020 Olympic Games, which were held in 2021 due to the COVID-19 pandemic, skateboarding was included for the first time in the history of the Games.

There were two skateboarding modalities in competition: street and park.

In the street competition, skaters perform tricks on a course that is similar to an urban environment, with obstacles such as stairs, rails, and curbs.

The goal is to perform technical and creative tricks using these obstacles, while moving around the course and demonstrating board control skills.

In the park competition, skaters compete on a course that resembles an empty swimming pool with curves and ramps.

Skaters move around the course performing tricks while jumping and spinning in the transitions between the curves and ramps.

The goal is to perform technical and creative tricks while taking advantage of the park's features to demonstrate board control and fluidity in movement.

Each competition has a limited time and competitors are judged based on the difficulty, style, and execution of the tricks.

Points are awarded based on the quality and difficulty of the tricks performed and the overall style of the execution.

21

The "Skate Board" by Roller Derby Skate Company was one of the first mass-produced skateboard models.

This model was manufactured in La Mirada, California, and began selling in 1963 during the first major skateboarding boom.

Unlike Alf Jensen's "Bun Board," which looked more like a surfboard with steel wheels, the "Skate Board" had a design more similar to modern skateboards, with a wooden deck, urethane wheels, and aluminum trucks.

Although it did not have bearings, it was very popular among young skaters at the time and helped popularize the sport across the United States.

Roller Derby Skate Company also produced other popular skateboard models in the following decades, such as the "Fireball" and "Super Surfer."

22

Linda Benson, born in 1944 in California, is a renowned surfer and skater in the history of board sports.

She was the first woman to grace the cover of a specialized surf magazine and has been an influential figure in the world of surfing and skateboarding.

As for skateboarding, Patti McGee, another California surfer, is recognized as the first professional female skateboarder.

In 1965, she won the first-ever women's skateboarding championship and was featured on the cover of LIFE magazine.

She is also known for being the first woman to skate on television on the show "The Price is Right."

Both Benson and McGee are important figures in the history of the sport and have paved the way for future generations of women in board sports.

23

The first skatepark in history was built in Tucson, Arizona in 1965 and was called "Surf City".

It was owned by Arizona Surf City Enterprises and was opened on September 3 of that year.

Patti McGee, one of the first women skaters, was present at the opening.

This skatepark was the first to offer skaters a suitable and specially designed surface to skate on.

In Spain, the first skatepark arrived in 1979 and was located in Arenys de Mar, in the province of Barcelona.

From there, several skateparks were built in different Spanish cities.

Nowadays, there are numerous skateparks all over the world, and they have become popular places for skaters to practice and show their skills on different types of obstacles and ramps.

In addition, skateparks have also allowed for the organization of skateboarding competitions, which have become increasingly popular worldwide.

24

The first skateboarding championship on record was held in Hermosa Beach, California in 1963 and was sponsored by the brand Makaha.

This event marked the beginning of competition in the world of skateboarding and skaters began to measure their skills in different disciplines such as slalom and freestyle.

From then on, more competitions and events were organized at the local and regional level, which allowed skateboarding to become a more popular sport worldwide.

Nowadays, there are worldwide skateboarding competitions such as the X Games and the Street League Skateboarding.

25

Skateboard wheels are a key element in the history and evolution of skateboarding.

In the 1950s, they began to be mass-produced and made of metal, but it was soon discovered that they were not suitable due to their lack of grip and limited durability.

In the 1960s, the change was made to clay wheels, which improved speed but were still difficult to control.

It was in the 1970s when Frank Nasworthy invented urethane wheels, which revolutionized the world of skateboarding.

These wheels offered greater grip and durability, allowing skaters to perform more advanced tricks and making skateboarding a more accessible discipline.

Since then, urethane wheels have become an essential element in skateboarding, and their design and technology have evolved to meet the needs of modern skaters.

26

During the drought of 1975 in California, the lack of water in the private pools of the area's houses allowed skaters of the time, especially in Venice Beach, to use them for skating.

It was then that the style of skateboarding known as "pool riding" or "vert skating" emerged, which involved skating inside empty pools and performing tricks on the walls.

The pioneering skaters of this modality were the members of the Zephyr team, better known as the "Lords of Dogtown," who revolutionized the world of skateboarding in the 1970s with their radical and gravity-defying style.

27

The first ever 900 in the history of skateboarding was performed at the 1999 X-Games by none other than Tony Hawk himself.

The trick involved completing two and a half spins in the air before landing back on the board.

It was a historic moment for skateboarding and for Tony Hawk, who had been working on that trick for years.

Additionally, in that same year, the first video game in the Tony Hawk's Pro Skater series was released for the PlayStation console, which became an instant hit and helped further popularize skateboarding.

Since then, Tony Hawk has continued to be an influential figure in the world of skateboarding, not only as a skater, but also as a business owner, philanthropist, and advocate for the sport.

28

Thrasher Magazine is a skateboarding magazine founded in San Francisco, California in 1981.

It is considered one of the most influential and respected publications in skateboarding culture.

The magazine covers a variety of topics related to skateboarding, including news, interviews, photos of both famous and unknown skaters, and opinion articles.

Additionally, every year it organizes the Skater of the Year (SOTY) event, which awards the most outstanding skater of the year.

Thrasher Magazine is also known for its iconic logo, which features the word "Thrasher" in bold font over a flame.

The logo has been reproduced on all kinds of skate products and clothing, becoming a symbol of skateboarding culture.

Additionally, the magazine has been mentioned in several punk rock and hip-hop songs, and has appeared in movies and TV shows.

29

What goal do you pursue with skateboarding?

To answer this simple question, it is essential to ask yourself: why or where do I want to skate?

If you are a surfer and want to recreate the movement of waves, then a surfskate is for you; if you want to move around the city, then a Penny board may suit you; if you want to do tricks, then a "standard" skateboard, which has been the most common since the late 90s, is for you; and if you are not sure about the terrain you will be on, make sure it is versatile, such as a longboard with softer and larger wheels, known as a cruiser.

30

A good quality skateboard costs around $100.

If you avoid getting it wet or leaving it outdoors for many days, you can keep your board in perfect condition.

At this price and being a beginner, the board can last you for more than a year without any problems.

Some recognized skateboard brands that you may come across during your search are Santa Cruz, Baker, Element, Girl, Flip, Blind, Zero, Birdhouse, Real, Toy Machine, or the Spanish brand Jart.

The list could be endless, so if you see any other brand, do not be surprised, but make sure to check if it is a well-known brand in the sector.

31

The board with the most suitable measurements.

A good option for beginners may be to
consider their shoe size.

For example, for a standard board, if you have
small feet, 7.5 is ideal, if you have between 40-42
then measurements between 7.9 and 8.25 may
work great for you, and if you are very tall
and/or big, then it is better to choose
a board between 8.1 and 8.5.

Also, keep in mind that the wider the board,
the better the balance, but it will be
harder to do tricks.

Thus, larger sizes are mainly used for ramps or
as a means of transportation, while smaller
sizes are used for freestyle.

Another factor to consider is the shape.

For this, you should go back to point one
and choose the shape that suits your goal.

32

Many skaters carry a "T" key with them while they skate.

This tool is essential for adjusting the nuts that hold the wheels and trucks of the board. It is also common for them to carry spare bearings in case one breaks during the skating session.

Bearings are the parts that allow the wheels to rotate around the axle, so if one is damaged, the wheel will not rotate correctly.

Having spares on hand can save a skating session.

In addition to these tools, skaters also often carry wax to slide better on rough surfaces and knee and elbow pads to prevent injuries.

33

What wheels are best suited to my skateboard and my skating style?

Doubts about wheels are multiple and
the options when buying, too.

The first thing to know is that practically all
skateboard wheels manufactured today are
made of polyurethane, a material that
is resistant to abrasion, has good grip,
and is cheap.

From here, three determining factors that are
usually indicated on each wheel must be taken
into account: 58mm – 20mm contact 101A.

In other words, diameter (58mm), a factor
related to the shape (20mm contact),
and hardness (101A).

34

The first thing to look at when it comes to skateboard wheels is indicated in millimeters, and roughly speaking, the following can be stated: the larger the size, the faster the speed and the easier it is to enter and exit when grinding obstacles; the smaller the size, the faster the acceleration and the better performance and control in technical tricks.

From here, we could say that the most common range is from 50 to 56mm.

From 50 to 53 are ideal for street skating because they are smaller, weigh less, and by having the skateboard lower and snapping tricks, it is faster.

The 53 could be said to be the most versatile.

From 53 to 56, on the other hand, they offer more speed and resistance to irregularities in the terrain, as well as for large curbs or handrails.

For beginners, it is recommended to buy wheels from 52 to 56mm.

Between 56 and 60 millimeters, which are already considered large wheels, they are also common for skating ramps.

They allow you to gain both speed and height and respond well to irregular terrain.

Finally, beyond 60, they would be wheels for longboards, cruisers, or surfskates.

35

It may seem like all wheels have the same shape, but that's not the case.

There are three types: Narrow: they have a narrower outer edge and therefore a smaller contact base with the ground, resulting in less friction and even when hitting and scraping the trick, they tend to spin from the first moment.

They are used for more technical street skating.

Wider: wider, more resistant and stable wheels, very versatile. Ideal for beginners, park, bowl, and fast skating.

Although they are also slightly rounded, it is not until the end.

For tricks on curbs, for example, they help to make the fit more perfect.

Classic: almost exclusively used for cruisers, practically rectangular if viewed from the front.

Full support of the wheel on the ground.

They weigh more but provide a lot of stability.

36

Polyurethane is a plastic that can have different degrees of hardness.

To measure it, a Durometer is used, which is nothing more than a scale with several categories that measure the hardness of plastics.

For skateboarding, the A scale is used, and the hardness usually ranges from 78A to 103A.

Some people use the B scale, which is simply the A scale minus 20 points (an 81B would be equivalent to a 101A).

In both cases, the higher the number, the harder the wheel.

Roughly speaking, it could be said that the harder a wheel is, the faster it is, the less grip it has, and therefore, better for ramps, skateparks, and technical tricks on more or less smooth terrain.

And more slide, if that's your interest.

On the other hand, the softer the wheel, the slower it is, the more grip it has, and optimal for a variety of terrains and irregularities such as rough asphalt or tiles.

Filmmakers, for example, use less hard wheels.

37

Texture.

It should be noted that the softer (or smooth) wheels are the most common and perfect for any type of skateboarding; but there are also other types of stickier (or sticky) wheels that grip better and even generate less noise; or those with treads, designed for non-smooth surfaces.

Finally, regarding color, a "curiosity": white wheels last longer because they do not contain dye and therefore the polyurethane is purer.

Never choose wheels based on color, but rather based on the first 3 criteria of size, hardness, and shape.

38

A skateboard is considered to be the one that measures around 32 inches (83 centimeters) in length by 8 inches (19-21 centimeters) in width, with a concave shape, and raised Nose and Tail that allow for performing tricks, the main function for which it was designed.

The trucks and wheels of the skateboard are usually hard and small, with a size of 5 inches (12 centimeters) for the former and a diameter ranging from 48 to 54 millimeters for the latter, with the same aim of facilitating tricks.

Its characteristics only allow for skating on hard and smooth surfaces, with the skatepark being the ideal place for it.

A good example is Richie Jackson, who does things with the skateboard that no one else can do.

39

The cruiser can be confused with a longboard or a skateboard because it has characteristics of both, but also has unique features.

The size is similar to that of a "modern" skateboard, but it has multiple shapes.

It is common to find it with only a tail to facilitate movements and some tricks, inspired by the models of the 70s, old school; but there are also those with Nose and concave shapes to facilitate tricks and moving in the bowl; and even plastic, flat ones, that are only for transportation.

In terms of the rest of the parts of the board, the cruiser's trucks are also small like those of a skateboard, but the wheels, on the other hand, are soft and slightly larger, ranging from 55 to 65 millimeters in diameter.

This type of board is designed for flat terrain or gentle hills and slopes, being a bit more versatile.

40

The longboard, or longboard skateboard, has a larger dimension than the previous two.

It is considered that anything over 36 inches (91 centimeters) is already a longboard.

The shapes are very varied depending on the use that is intended for it: with different concavities, with raised Nose and Tail for freestyle, with more lateral concavity for freeriding, with flex to make the board yield when stepping on it and facilitate dancing, etc.

The wheels are soft like those on a cruiser, although the size is even larger, ranging from 60 to 90 millimeters in diameter.

The trucks, in this case, are generally larger and higher.

41

The only complete and private collection of 20 years of "exclusive" Supreme skateboards, sold for $800,000.

In 2008, a passionate skate and art collector named Ryan Fuller from Los Angeles started collecting them.

Since they were difficult to access, he had to contact people from all over the world to complete his collection: Australia, South Africa, UK, Japan...

Fuller says that the ones from the first 10 years are the most difficult to obtain, because they were originally used for what they were created for: skating.

Thus, obtaining unused or unripped skateboards was almost impossible.

In this context, the most difficult one to find was the fifth board in the set of 5 Supreme skateboards in collaboration with artist Dan Colen "Air Jordan", released in 2003.

He had 4 of the 5 for years and thought that fifth one didn't even exist.

One day, while on vacation in Hawaii, a man he had done business with for years sent him an email saying that he had found it in his warehouse.

42

**The world's largest skateboard is known as
"The Big Boy" and has a length of 11.15 meters
and a width of 2.64 meters.**

It was built in 2009 by Joe Ciaglia and Rob Dyrdek
in a factory in Los Angeles, California.

The skateboard is so large that it takes at least 12 people
to move it and a specialized vehicle to transport it.

After its creation, "The Big Boy" has appeared in several
events and television programs, including
"Rob Dyrdek's Fantasy Factory" and "Nitro Circus".

Additionally, it has been rented out for special
events and has been used by some professional
skaters to perform tricks on it.

In 2015, the skateboard was exhibited at the California
Science Center in Los Angeles as part of an exhibition
called "The Art of the Brick", where artistic creations
made with Lego pieces were showcased.

The skateboard was covered with Lego pieces to
make it appear even larger and more striking.

"The Big Boy" has been recognized as the world's
largest skateboard by the Guinness World
Records since 2011.

43

Tony Hawk's likes and preferences.

His first inspiration: Eddie Elguera, the most innovative skater when he started.

Who he considers the best skater of all time: Rodney Mullen, almost all current skate tricks have been invented or inspired by him.

He thinks that the top skate cities in Europe are: Barcelona, Madrid, Paris, and London.

His perfect day: waking up with his kids, taking them to school, handling professional matters, calls, emails, interviews, and skateboarding!

His favorite place to skate: the ramp at his office.

The best company for skating: Kevin Staab, Andy McDonald, Elliot Sloan, Bucky Lasek, and Lance Mountain.

44

"Lords of Dogtown" is a 2005 sports drama film directed by Catherine Hardwicke.

It is based on a documentary called "Dogtown and Z-Boys" from 2001, which tells the story of the Zephyr skate team from Venice Beach, Los Angeles, California, in the 1970s.

The team, composed of Jay Adams, Tony Alva, Stacy Peralta, among others, are considered pioneers of modern skateboarding and the style of skating in empty swimming pools and surfing.

The film shows how this group of young, marginalized and rebellious people revolutionized the world of skateboarding in the 1970s, creating their own style and taking skateboarding from the streets to empty swimming pools.

It also explores themes such as friendship, rivalry, success, and failure, as well as the cultural and social impact of the skateboarding movement at that time.

The film features an outstanding cast, with Emile Hirsch playing Jay Adams, Victor Rasuk as Tony Alva, and John Robinson as Stacy Peralta.

Heath Ledger and Nikki Reed also appear in the film, among others.

"Lords of Dogtown" received mostly positive reviews and became a cult film for skate and street culture enthusiasts.

45

John Rodney Mullen, also known as "Rodney Mullen," is an influential and innovative professional skateboarder considered one of the greatest in the history of skateboarding.

He is known as the father of street skateboarding, as he was the first to take skateboarding tricks to the streets instead of limiting them to ramps.

Mullen started skating at the age of 10 and won his first skateboarding championship at the age of 14.

From then on, Mullen began winning various championships and was sponsored by different skateboarding brands.

In the 1980s and 1990s, Mullen invented a large number of tricks, many of which are still used today.

Some of his most famous tricks include the Kickflip, the Heelflip, the 360 Flip, the Casper Flip, and the Darkslide.

In addition to being a professional skateboarder, Mullen is also a mechanical engineer and has worked on the design of skateboards and other skateboarding equipment.

Currently, Mullen is retired from professional skateboarding, but he is still active in the community and is considered a legend and a source of inspiration for many skateboarders around the world.

46

Ryan Sheckler is a famous American professional skateboarder known for his aggressive skateboarding style and his skill in the street discipline.

He started skating at the age of 2, and by the age of 7, he was already winning competitions.

At the age of 13, he became the youngest skateboarder to win a gold medal at the X Games.

In his career, Ryan Sheckler has won numerous championships and competitions, including the Dew Tour, X Games, and Street League Skateboarding.

He has also appeared in several movies and television series, including his own reality show "Life of Ryan."

In addition to his skateboarding career, Sheckler has participated in charity work and founded his own charitable organization, the Sheckler Foundation, which is dedicated to helping children and young people in need through skateboarding and other sports activities.

Sheckler has also been sponsored by several major skateboarding brands, such as Etnies, Plan B Skateboards, and Red Bull, among others.

47

Paul Rodriguez Jr., also known as P-Rod, is one of the most influential and successful skaters in the history of professional skateboarding.

He was born in Tarzana, California on December 31, 1984 and is the son of the famous comedian Paul Rodriguez Sr.

He started skating at the age of 12 and quickly caught the attention of the skateboarding industry.

In 2002, at the age of 18, he turned professional and since then he has won numerous championships and competitions, including X Games, Street League Skateboarding, and Dew Tour.

In addition to his skateboarding career, Paul Rodriguez has had some roles in movies and TV shows, including "Wild Grinders" and "Street Dreams".

He has also been sponsored by several brands, including Nike SB and Plan B Skateboards, and has launched his own line of skate clothing and shoes.

Paul Rodriguez is considered a skateboarding legend and has influenced an entire generation of skaters around the world.

48

**Chris Cole is an American professional skater
born in Langhorne, Pennsylvania.**

He started skating at the age of 9 and by the time he
was 18 he was already a professional skater.

Throughout his career, he has achieved numerous titles,
including two gold medals at the X Games, and has been one
of the most influential skaters in the skateboarding scene.

Cole is known for his aggressive and technical style in his
skating, and has invented several tricks that bear his name,
such as the "Cole Flip" and the "Heelflip Indy 900".

He has been sponsored by brands like Zero Skateboards,
Fallen Footwear, DC Shoes, Monster Energy,
and Spitfire Wheels.

In addition to his career as a professional skater, Cole has
been involved in several skateboarding-related film projects,
such as the documentary "Rising Son: The Legend
of Skateboarder Christian Hosoi" and the movie
"Street Dreams".

He has also appeared in skateboarding video games such
as the "Tony Hawk's Pro Skater" series and "Skate".

In recent years, Cole has been involved in projects to
promote inclusivity and diversity in skateboarding,
and has publicly spoken about his struggles with
addiction to drugs and alcohol.

49

Skate punk is a subgenre of punk rock that is given by the proximity that punk music has had with skateboarding at different times.

This term is commonly used for early 90s melodic hardcore bands and later groups with a similar sound.

The beginnings of punk culture and the rise of skateboarding in the United States coincide in the same time and place: California.

Therefore, these two cultures, which were quite underground at first, were destined to understand each other.

In this way, skaters began to attend concerts and buy punk records.

At the same time, many punk band members adopted skate and surf culture as their own.

Examples of the first groups that could fit into this style would be bands like Minor Threat, Black Flag, 7 Seconds, The Adolescents, Dead Kennedys, or Circle Jerks.

50

Video Games:

Skate Boarding Atari 2600 ·
Absolute Entertainment · 1987.

David Crane brought us this
poorly made mess, considered
the first attempt to make
skateboarding games.

In five minutes, you had to do as many
tricks as possible (there were 30
different ones) between tubes, fences,
and ramps, on an empty street and
with a jump button that was useless.

51

As the skater himself has defined, Tony Hawk was a very complicated kid, suffering from hyperactivity and having a very high level of self-demand.

There came a point where his parents, desperate with the situation, decided to take their son to a psychologist to try to understand the situation they were experiencing.

During these visits, the psychologist revealed to Hawk's parents that the child had a mindset ahead of his age, that of an adult.

Tony's success is due to the fact that since he was eight years old, he never stopped practicing in the skateparks closest to his house with his skateboard.

His skills were so great that at the age of 12, he already had his own agent, at 14 he was already a professional, and at 16, the best skater in the world.

Along with his brother, he founded the California Amateur League and the National Skateboard Association.

52

Tony Hawk started skating thanks to his brother Danny, who in 1977 gave him his first skateboard with the intention of trying to improve the hyperactive situation Tony was experiencing.

It was with that skateboard that from that moment on he began to practice this sport until he fully dedicated himself to it.

53

What tricks has Tony Hawk invented?

In his long career, this skateboarder achieved
numerous accomplishments that
few are indifferent to.

By 2004, Hawk had more than 10 victories
and several tricks of his own invention in his
resume, such as the "Madonna," "Benihana,"
"Stalefish," and variations of the
famous "Airwalk."

On the other hand, he has also stood out as
the first to achieve a "720" (two rotations)
when he was only 17 years old.

In 1999, at 43 years old, he performed a "900"
(two and a half rotations) thanks to practicing
relentlessly for 10 years.

54

When practicing any sport, but especially one like skateboarding where jumps and stunts are the order of the day, it is normal for athletes to suffer injuries.

Hawk is no exception, and despite numerous falls experienced by the skater, undoubtedly the worst was the one that left him unable to participate in competitions for a year due to a broken pelvis, a broken thumb, and a fractured skull.

Another problem for the skater came in the early 90s when he mismanaged his expenses and squandered most of the millions he had earned skating, surviving on only 5 dollars a day.

Fortunately, with the founding of Birdhouse and the release of video games, he was able to recover his finances.

He also created Hawk Clothing, a skate apparel and footwear company that would eventually be acquired by Quiksilver.

55

During his childhood, Tony Hawk also excelled at playing the violin.

His father was a jazz musician and taught him to play the instrument at an early age.

Hawk combined his violin lessons with his skate training, but eventually had to choose between the two due to lack of time.

According to some interviews, the decision was not difficult, as he was more interested in skateboarding.

Despite his choice, Hawk has not completely abandoned music.

In fact, he has played guitar and bass in several bands, including his own band called "Birdhouse."

He has also been a DJ at some events and has collaborated on the soundtrack of some skateboarding-related video games.

56

How many times has Tony Hawk appeared on television?

This famous athlete has appeared on television more than 20 times.

One of the first times he did so was in the movie "Police Academy 4" in which he played a skateboarder.

In addition, he has been seen in scenes from the "Jackass" series and movies, as well as in other more dramatic productions such as "CSI: Crime Scene Investigation" or lending his voice to productions such as "Phineas and Ferb."

He has also achieved certain personal recognitions, especially in 2009 when Barack Obama invited him to the White House, allowing him to skateboard inside it.

On the other hand, Transworld Skateboarding magazine named him the second most notable skateboarder in history and Fox Weekly named him one of the world's best skaters.

57

According to Tony Hawk himself, the craziest thing he has ever done was jump with his skateboard between two seven-story buildings in the city of Los Angeles for a program on the MTV channel.

Talent has nothing to do with age and Tony Hawk has always wanted to make this very clear.

Despite being a professional at 14 and the best skateboarder in the world at 16, he never settled and continued trying new things with the aim of surpassing himself.

He did a "900" at 43 for the first time and at 48 decided he wanted to perfect it, and of course he did.

Hawk is a role model for success, overcoming obstacles, and perseverance, which according to him, has led him to become the unbeatable athlete who, after so many decades, continues to be the idol of more than one generation.

58

How much does it cost to make a custom complete skateboard?

· **Deck:** it is the most important part of your custom skateboard, as it refers to the base where you will be standing when doing your skate tricks and what ultimately holds your body. It usually costs between €30 and €45.

· **Trucks:** you should not skimp on the trucks, as they are a vital aspect for riding the skateboard. They generally cost €15–€30.

· **Wheels:** the wheels are also among the most important components of the skateboard. Without them, the skateboard does not move. It should be noted that the price of skateboard wheels varies depending on the size, material, and shape. On average, they usually cost between €15 and €35.

· **Bearings:** these are vital parts of the skateboard, especially if you plan to have the board move and roll without having to constantly push. As for bearings, expect to pay around €18–€140, as you can see, a wide price range.

· **Hardware:** generally composed of nuts and bolts that are essential for securing the truck to the deck. When purchasing hardware, buy them in packs of 8 items. Each set usually costs around €4–€10.

59

It was in the 1960s when the skateboarding movement and its popularity grew significantly, and the first companies dedicated to making these four-wheeled skates emerged.

Brands such as Jack's, Hobie, and Makaha came to light, and even competitions began to be held.

They were not like the skateboarding competitions we know today, back then, what was popular was slalom and freestyle.

And obviously a basic freestyle, without the skateboarding tricks and genius moves we know today.

At the end of the 60s, the opposite effect mysteriously occurred, and the skateboarding movement declined again, and only a few people continued to skate, with their rudimentary skateboards, which were very dangerous and difficult to control.

60

In the 1970s, skateboarding had lost its popularity and was on the decline.

However, in 1973, Frank Nasworthy invented urethane wheels, which revolutionized the skateboarding industry and led to a resurgence of the sport.

Before this, skate wheels were made of clay or metal and were hard, making skating difficult and dangerous.

Urethane wheels were softer and more durable, allowing for better control and maneuverability on the skateboard.

Nasworthy also founded a company called Cadillac Wheels to produce and sell these wheels.

The invention of urethane wheels contributed to the rebirth of skateboarding and opened up new possibilities for the sport.

61

1980s: The birth of modern skateboarding.

We could say that modern skateboarding as we know it today was born in this decade.

During this time, there was a great evolution in terms of skateboard manufacturing materials and the tricks performed on them.

Vert skateboarding experienced spectacular growth during this era, as did the Street style.

This period saw the so-called golden age of skateboarding, as super important brands emerged such as Powell Peralta, Vision, Santa Cruz, Independent, and others.

Thanks to the rise of VHS videos, many skateboarding events and recordings were produced, and the dissemination of this material helped spread the sport even further.

The legendary Bones Brigade team also emerged during this time, whose videos marked a turning point due to the spectacular nature of their moves and tricks.

This team included skateboarding legends such as Tony Hawk, Steve Caballero, Rodney Mullen, Lance Mountain, Stacy Peralta, Mike McGill, and more.

62

**In the early 90s, the popularity of
skateboarding once again declined.**

Skateboarders were associated with the
underground style, so they had
a bad reputation.

Street style developed greatly,
while Vert declined for years.

During this time, thousands of young people
hit the streets to perform their skate
tricks and have fun on their boards.

The shape of the boards was modified until it
became similar to the current shape, while
the size of the wheels was reduced,
achieving better control of the boards.

63

2000s: Skateboarding solidifies as a sport.

During this time, an important event
occurred: the X-Games were held.

Thanks to this event, skateboarding
experienced a very important boost and
many people began to admire it even more.

This event marked the association of
skateboarding as a sport and spectacle.

Skateboarding was everywhere: on TV,
in video games, in parks...

And all of this brought with it that many
important people with money saw
skateboarding as a business opportunity to
exploit, so skateboarding grew even more.

Lots of skate parks dedicated to
skateboarders were created
all over the world.

64

How to ride a skateboard?

Like any progression, the first step to learning how to ride a skateboard is getting used to the sensation of the board.

To do this, we need to position ourselves on a smooth and comfortable surface.

Make sure your front foot is placed between the two front wheels and your back foot is placed between the two back wheels, on the surface on top of the wheels.

It is this fact that provides balance.

Try to bend your knees and jump a bit, and move forward and backward, from the edge of your foot to the edge of your heel and back, feeling the rigidity of the skateboard and the basic movements of the board.

65

The prohibition of skateboarding sales in Norway between 1978 and 1989 is an interesting historical fact in skateboarding culture.

It is said that the reason for the prohibition was that skateboarding caused damage to urban furniture, which was considered a problem for the Norwegian community and government.

The ban did not include the practice of skateboarding itself, but simply the sale of skateboards.

The prohibition led Norwegian skaters to build their own ramps in isolated places, such as forests and other places with little police presence, in order to practice.

Despite the ban, skateboarding remained popular in Norway, and skaters found creative ways to continue practicing their sport.

The prohibition was finally lifted in 1989, when Norwegian authorities realized that the ban was not working and that skateboarding remained popular.

Since then, skateboarding has continued to grow in popularity in Norway and around the world.

66

There is no official and up-to-date source that provides a list of countries with the number of registered skaters.

However, according to a 2019 market research study of the skateboarding industry, the United States, Japan, and Brazil are the top three skateboarding markets in terms of market value and consumption of skate-related products.

It is also worth noting that the American Sports Data estimated that worldwide, 84% of skaters are under 18 years old, of which 74% are male and 26% are female.

67

In recent years, there has been a shift in the way skaters and the community as a whole are perceived.

It is becoming more common to see female skaters, and inclusion and diversity are gaining ground in the skateboarding industry.

Skateboarding has become more accessible to everyone, and there is a greater selection of clothing and gear aimed at women and people from different ethnic and cultural backgrounds.

Furthermore, with the inclusion of skateboarding in the Olympics, it is expected that the visibility of skaters and the sport in general will increase even further, and that the community will continue to grow and evolve in a more inclusive and equitable direction.

Brands like "Monarch Project" are leading this change, promoting inclusion and gender equality in skateboarding and working to create a more positive and safe environment for all skaters, regardless of their gender, sexual orientation, race, or religion.

68

Kahlei Stone-Kelly hasn't even taken off his diapers yet, but he can ride a scooter like a pro.

This two-year-old Australian boy has become a sensation on Youtube after his father recorded him on the board and uploaded the video.

Born into a family of skaters who compete all over the world, Kahlei started practicing with the scooter at six months old, according to his parents' statements to The Mirror newspaper.

His success has been such that his parents have decided to open a Facebook page for him, so that fans can follow his progress.

They have posted several videos showing the little one's stunts; he jumps curbs, does spins, takes turns at high speeds, and all without any protection other than his diaper, which is also being heavily criticized on social media.

69

Those who have seen the movie Back to the Future II probably remember the hoverboard that Michael J. Fox and the bad guys use in a chase.

Well, it seems that a company has developed a technology based on levitation through magnetic fields and one of its first projects is the prototype of this curious hoverboard, which has managed to lift off the ground by creating a magnetic field.

According to media such as The Verge and Re/code, which were able to test the experience, the board effectively hovers over the ground, achieving a lift of about 3 centimeters.

And although it can be used, at the moment it is far from being as manageable as in the movie and can only be used on conductive surfaces, such as copper.

70

Skateboarding enthusiasts now have a new "toy," OneWheel, an electric skateboard with a single wheel.

A team of American engineers has presented a new skateboard that is controlled by body tilt and has a single central wheel.

This group of entrepreneurs has wanted to transfer the sensations of snowboarding to the pavement with this kind of electric skateboard that accelerates when the user leans in one direction and brakes when he or she leans in the opposite direction.

71

When a skateboard gets wet, water can penetrate the wood and affect its internal structure.

Wood swells when it gets wet and then shrinks when it dries, which can cause the layers of the board to separate or crack.

In addition, moisture can weaken the glue that holds the layers together, which can make the board break more easily.

In general, it is recommended not to skate on wet surfaces as it can not only affect the board but also be dangerous for the skater due to the risk of slips and falls.

If the skateboard gets wet, it is best to let it dry completely before using it again to avoid any long-term problems.

72

In skateboarding competitions, there are two main categories: Skate Street and Skate Bowl.

The Skate Street discipline takes place on a course that simulates urban elements such as stairs, handrails, benches, ledges, and other obstacles.

Skaters have to demonstrate their ability to jump, slide, and perform tricks on these street elements, and they are evaluated based on difficulty, creativity, style, and technique.

On the other hand, the Skate Bowl discipline takes place on a course with a bowl or empty swimming pool shape, with curved walls and smooth transitions, where skaters perform aerial tricks and tricks over the edges.

Bowls are usually made of concrete, and their size can vary according to the level of skaters participating.

In this type of competition, judges evaluate the fluidity, style, creativity, and height of the tricks performed by participants.

73

Evaluation criteria in competition.

Each category is judged with different criteria, but in general, it penalizes repeating tricks and having a conservative repertoire.

Skate competition judges try to find a balance between coherence and creativity.

Judges score individual timed runs based on the following parameters:

-Use of the entire course.

-Difficulty and technique of the tricks.

-Execution (clean landings).

-Variety of tricks.

-Speed, fluidity, and style.

-Consistency (absence of errors).

74

What are the essential movements and techniques in skateboarding?

Ollie: The ollie is a hands-free aerial movement achieved by hitting the tail of the board against the ground and guiding the rebound in the air solely with the traction of the foot.

Shove It: An ollie where the tail hits the ground at a 45-degree angle, causing the energy of the hit to spin the board 180 degrees laterally beneath the skater's feet.

Kickflip: an ollie where the front foot spins the board longitudinally in a full rotation.

Heelflip: Essentially, a kickflip in the opposite direction.

Grinds/slides: It's the use of different sections of the skateboard, either the board (slides) or the metal trucks (grinds) to ride along the edges of an obstacle.

Nollie: An ollie that uses the nose of the board instead of the tail.

Grabs: The art of grabbing the skateboard in mid-air is more a matter of style than necessity.

Switchstance: It's not so much a trick as a reversal of form: the "switch" involves riding backward, i.e., mounting in the opposite direction of regular stance.

75

Events.

-Street League Skateboarding: The international series of street competitions.

-Vans Park Series: The ultimate bowl series, where skateparks are often built for the event and then donated to the host city.

-Red Bull Bowl Rippers: Annual aerial combat at the historic Bowl Du Prado, in fabulous Marseille.

-Tampa Am/Pro: The most democratic way to make a name for oneself in competitive skateboarding is in Tampa, where the eyes of industry giants are fixed.

-Vans Pool Party: Takes place at the Vans Combi Pool in Orange County, California, and is the ideal place to find out who's who in concrete.

-X Games: In its 25th year, the first action sports festival made for television still attracts the biggest names in competitive skateboarding.

76

Hawk has lived through uncomfortable situations.

One of them happened at an airport, when an agent checked his ID.

"Your last name is Hawk, like the skater Tony Hawk. I wonder what happened to him," the officer said without realizing he had the celebrity right in front of him.

Similarly, it happened to him again at another checkpoint, when an agent commented, "I'm trying to figure out who you look like before I see your passport... That cyclist Armstrong! Oh no, you look like that skater and even have the same last name. How crazy!"

However, Hawk has had other experiences in other public places, such as a gas station, where someone asked him, "Have you ever been told that you look like Tony Hawk, but younger?" or in a store, when a kid asked him if he wasn't often mistaken for Tony Hawk.

77

The Burnside Skatepark is an iconic skatepark located under the Burnside Bridge in Portland, Oregon, United States.

It was built by local skaters led by Mark "Red" Scott in the 1990s.

The location was chosen due to its protection from rain, which allowed local skaters to enjoy skateboarding year-round.

The construction of the skatepark was largely a community effort, and local skaters worked hard to build and maintain it.

The city of Portland initially tried to destroy it, but the skateboarding community organized protests, and eventually, an agreement was reached to keep the skatepark.

The Burnside Skatepark has become a popular destination for skaters from all over the world and has been home to important skateboarding competitions.

Additionally, it has been a source of inspiration for other skaters and for the creation of other DIY skateparks around the world.

78

Southbank is an area located in London, England that has become an iconic spot for skaters since the 1960s.

This area is home to a large number of obstacles for practicing street skateboarding, such as stairs, railings, curbs, benches, and ledges.

In 2004, the London public transportation company, Transport for London (TFL), proposed the demolition of the Southbank skatepark to build a bus station, which generated controversy among skaters and the general public.

Skaters organized and launched a campaign to save the skatepark, which led to the then-mayor of London, Boris Johnson, intervening and ensuring that the space would be preserved for skaters.

After several years of negotiations, an agreement was reached in 2014 to renovate and update the Southbank skatepark, which included restoring the original obstacles and building new areas to skate.

Today, Southbank is one of the most iconic and popular spots for skaters in Europe and is visited by skateboarders from all over the world.

79

The Big O is an iconic skatepark located in Montreal, Canada.

Originally, the site was a stadium built for the 1976 Summer Olympics, but after the games, the stadium remained abandoned for many years.

In the 1990s, local skaters discovered that the stadium's entrance tunnel, known as the "Big O," was a perfect spot for skating due to its smooth curves and transitions.

Over time, skaters built their own ramps and obstacles at the location, creating a unique skatepark that has been praised by skateboarders from all over the world.

The Big O has hosted numerous skateboarding events and is considered one of the best places to skate in Canada.

80

MACBA (Museu d'Art Contemporani de Barcelona) is one of the most famous skate spots in Europe and the world.

It is located in the Raval neighborhood of Barcelona, Spain, and was opened in 1995.

The plaza features a large smooth marble surface and multiple stairs, benches, and curbs that are ideal for skateboarding.

Since its opening, MACBA has become a meeting point for skaters from Barcelona and around the world, and has been the venue for prestigious skateboarding competitions and events.

Additionally, in the vicinity of MACBA, other famous places for skating can be found, such as the Balmes plaza and the Fórum park.

The city of Barcelona has become a very popular destination among skaters due to the large number and variety of spots it offers, as well as its warm and sunny climate for much of the year.

81

Kona Skatepark is located in Jacksonville, Florida, and was founded in 1977.

It was built by the Ramos brothers, who opened it to the public as a place for skaters to enjoy the sport.

The park has a wide variety of ramps, bowls, and obstacles, and has become a very popular place for both local skaters and visitors from around the world.

In addition to being the world's oldest privately owned skatepark, Kona Skatepark is famous for its role in skate culture.

Many professional skaters have skated here, and it has been the site of numerous events and competitions.

It has also appeared in several skateboarding video games, including the Tony Hawk's Pro Skater series.

Over the years, Kona Skatepark has faced some challenges, such as financial problems and damage from hurricanes, but it remains a popular destination for skateboarding enthusiasts.

The Ramos family has kept the park running for over 40 years, and it remains an important place in the history of skateboarding.

82

Red Ribbon (China) Did you imagine finding a skate paradise in China?

Well, they know how to enjoy it here too.

Guangzhou is considered a skate paradise by professional skaters who are willing to travel the world to get here.

Its unique structure has become a great challenge for many skaters around the world.

83

The Pink Motel Pool is an empty swimming pool located in Sun Valley, California, United States, that has become an iconic spot for skateboarders.

It was built in the 1940s as part of a motel called "Pink Motel", but after the motel closed, the pool was left abandoned and empty.

In the 1980s, skaters discovered the pool and began using it to skate.

Since then, it has become a popular spot for skaters from around the world, and has appeared in several skate videos and documentaries.

Currently, the Pink Motel Pool is a private skate spot, but some events and competitions have been organized there in the past.

84

Landhausplatz is a plaza located in the historic center of Innsbruck, Austria, and features a skatepark designed by Rudi-Josef Altig, an architect who is passionate about skateboarding.

The park is well-known for its unique style and design, which combine elements of classical and modern architecture.

In the past, there were some conflicts between skaters and pedestrians, as the plaza is a popular meeting place for citizens and tourists.

However, there is now an agreement between the parties to share the space and maintain safety for all users.

In addition to being a popular destination for skaters, Landhausplatz is also an important tourist spot due to its historic buildings and impressive architecture.

85

Sky Brown: the 12-year-old girl who participated in the Olympics and is a professional skateboarder.

From a young age, she was interested in the sport.

YouTube videos also helped her perfect certain details that have led her to the biggest sports event.

At the age of 8, she competed in the Vans US Open, becoming the youngest person to compete in the event.

In 2018, she was part of the Vans Park series and ranked in the top 10.

However, Sky Brown's fame began to show when she won the American show Dancing with the Stars: Juniors.

In 2019, she participated in the Skateboarding World Championship where she won bronze.

That same year, she became the first female skateboarder to perform a Frontside 540 during the X Games.

86

Nyjah Huston has over $6 million.

Nyjah Huston, a professional skateboarder and five-time champion of the Street League Skateboarding competition series, is the world's highest-paid skateboarder.

Although he appears at the end of our list, this is only because he has not had enough time in his career to truly build his wealth or brand.

It's not that he lacks experience; Huston started skating at the age of four.

Nyjah Huston has officially won more money in skateboarding competitions than any other skater.

He has also been named the fifth most influential skater of all time on a FoxWeekly list.

This 23-year-old sports star has already made a considerable fortune; it's only a matter of time before he expands into his own brand and business.

87

Mike Carroll won $6 million.

Michael Shawn Carroll is one of the world's leading skateboarders and skateboarding entrepreneurs.

He is vice president and co-founder of Girl Skateboards, and even played a founding role in the creation of Lakai Limited Footwear.

His favorite project was Girl's Chocolate Skateboards division, which soon grew to take a significant part of the market.

He is also known for his skate technique and style, which is showcased in some videos like Video Days, Hokus Pokus, and Ban This.

This man has earned every penny of the money he has today.

He has also won some awards as a skater, including the Skater of the Year award from Thrasher magazine.

He won it in 1994 at the age of 19.

Mike Carroll has also been selected as one of the most influential skaters, ranking sixteenth on a Transworld Skateboarding list called The 30 Most Influential Skaters of All Time.

88

**Andy Macdonald earned
6 million dollars.**

This Massachusetts native started
in 1986 at the age of twelve.

Although he started a little later than
many other skaters, his career
and talent were not affected
in the slightest.

He is an avid competitor in the X
Games and holds the world record for
vertical skateboarding for the most
medals won in the X Games
in a single year.

He is also an eight-time winner of the
Skateboarding World Cup competition.

89

Bob Burnquist earned 8 million dollars.

This skater is a citizen of both Brazil and the United States.

He was born in Rio de Janeiro and began training in his hometown of Sao Paulo at the age of eleven.

It only took him 3 years to become a professional, being officially sponsored at the age of 14.

He is a well-known skater in vertical skateboarding, even in the X Games and some other competitions.

Bob Burnquist has many signature tricks.

The most famous is the "fakie 900," which features a natural reverse rotation of 900 degrees.

This made Bob the fifth person to complete a 900-degree spin and the first to do it in fakie.

Burnquist has also won many gold medals and is among the most recognized skaters in the world.

90

Stacy Peralta earned 10 million dollars.

Stacy Peralta was a key influential figure
in promoting the early skate culture.

He started at the age of fifteen, competing
alongside the Z-Boys (also known
as the Zephyr Competition Team).

They were sponsored by Jeff Ho Surfboards
and Zephyr Productions and were a key group
in the skate culture of the 1970s.

He has also advanced a lot in skate
culture and entertainment.

The first "frontside lip slide to fakie" was
completed by Peralta sometime in the 70s,
making him the inventor of this trick.

For a short time, he was the highest-ranked
professional skater and eventually
formed the Bones Brigade.

91

Mike Vallely earned $10,000,000.

He started at the age of 14.

He got his first skateboard from a friend and quickly embraced the mid-1980s punk-focused skate scene.

He then decided to dedicate his life to skateboarding and has since progressed in both urban and vertical styles.

His first step towards success was at Mount Trashmore, a skatepark in Virginia Beach, where he started skating with some friends in view of the pros.

Soon, Mike V was offered his first sponsorship contract with Powell-Peralta Skateboards.

His career took off quickly, and he soon became a household name in professional skateboarding.

92

Lance Mountain earned $10,000,000.

Robert Lance Mountain, better known as Lance, is an artist and a skateboarder who rose to fame in the Bones Brigade era of the 1980s.

He started in Pasadena, California, in the early days of skateboarding.

To this day, he continues to skate professionally, even at the age of 53.

He is also known for being instrumental in the invention of the fingerboard, like the popular Tech Deck mini boards that were made for a while.

93

Ed Templeton earned $10,000,000.

Professional skateboarder, contemporary artist, and entrepreneur Ed Templeton is a current resident of Huntington Beach, California.

Templeton did not have a very long professional career.

He skated for New Deal Skateboards from 1990 to 1992, when he left to found his own companies.

Despite his short professional career, he is considered the twentieth most influential skater of all time by Skateboarding Transworld.

94

Andrew Reynolds earned $10,000,000.

This professional skateboarder, a prolific embracer of the urban style, is the co-founder and owner of Baker Skateboards.

He also has a stake in Bakerboys Distribution and Brigade Eyewear.

He also holds the prominent position of chief designer at Altamont Apparel.

He won Thrasher's Skater of the Year in 1998.

He also held it in 2010, with a Transworld Skateboarding Video Part of the Year award in 2011.

He also appears in many Tony Hawk games.

95

Wee Man earned $12,000,000.

This skateboarder was born as Jason Shannon Acuña but is commonly known by the nickname "Wee Man".

He was born in Pisa, Italy and grew up in California. His career did not start on the streets, but in association with a magazine called Big Brother.

He gained fame for his involvement in the MTV television series "Jackass" and the movies that derived from it.

Additionally, he has appeared on other television shows such as "Arrested Development" and "C.S.I.". As for his skateboarding career, Wee Man has won several awards and competitions, including the "Slam City Jam" and the "World Cup of Skateboarding".

He has also been sponsored by companies like Element Skateboards and Adio Footwear.

He owns a Chronic Tacos in Redondo Beach, California and has also been a host for Fox Sports, on a skate show.

96

Danny Way earned $12,000,000.

One of the most famous skateboarders
in the world is Danny Way.

He is best known as the pioneer of megaramps,
and even used one to jump the Great Wall
of China on his skateboard.

He was born in Portland, Oregon and
had a difficult upbringing.

He channeled his frustrations through
skateboarding and quickly made a name
for himself in the scene.

In addition to his stunts, Danny Way is
also known for co-founding Plan B,
a skateboarding company.

He has also won many awards, since he entered
his first contest and won at the age of eleven.

His incredible fortune is the result of hard work.

97

The International Skateboarding Federation (ISF) was founded in 2004 and was dedicated to promoting and organizing skateboarding events at an international level, including world and regional championships.

However, in September 2017, the ISF merged with the International Roller Sports Federation (FIRS) to form World Skate, an organization that is responsible for the promotion and organization of skating events in all its disciplines, including skateboarding, roller skating, artistic skating, and roller hockey, among others.

World Skate is recognized by the International Olympic Committee (IOC) as the governing body for skateboarding in the Olympic context.

98

Street League Skateboarding (SLS) is a professional skateboarding league founded in 2010 by skater and entrepreneur Rob Dyrdek.

The league's goal is to create an exciting competition format for street skateboarding, which in turn attracts more skaters and increases the sport's popularity.

The best skaters in the world compete in SLS, including names like Nyjah Huston, Shane O'Neill, and Leticia Bufoni.

The competition is divided into several stages and culminates in a world championship where the top 8 skaters in the ranking compete for the $1.6 million cash prize, which is the highest economic prize in the history of skateboarding.

SLS has been responsible for boosting the popularity and recognition of skateboarding worldwide, and has helped bring the sport to a higher level of professionalism and respect.

In addition to live events, SLS also has an online presence with videos, social media, and live broadcasts of competitions.

99

The World Cup of Skateboarding (WCS) is an organization dedicated to the promotion and organization of international skateboarding events.

It was founded in 1994 by the United States' National Skateboard Association (NSA) and has since been responsible for the organization of numerous competitions and events worldwide.

WCS sponsors a series of events in its ranking, which include street and vert skateboarding competitions, and feature some of the world's best professional skaters.

Additionally, the organization has significantly contributed to the growth and development of skateboarding as a sport and lifestyle, and has helped establish quality and safety standards for skateboarding events worldwide.

The World Cup of Skateboarding has also been responsible for creating some of the most important and influential events in skateboarding history, such as the Vans Triple Crown, the Gravity Games, and the Slam City Jam, among others.

These events have attracted thousands of spectators and have helped elevate the profile of skateboarding on an international level.

100

The Dew Tour is an annual skateboarding event held in the United States.

It is sponsored by the beverage brand Mountain Dew and has been an important platform for professional skaters to showcase their skills in various competitions, including street and park.

The event has evolved over the years and has incorporated new disciplines such as BMX and snowboarding.

In addition to the competition, there are also activities and exhibitions for spectators and skateboarding enthusiasts.

The location of the event varies each year, but some places where it has been organized include Long Beach, California, Breckenridge, Colorado, and Ocean City, Maryland.

101

Other events:

-**Vans Park Series.** The ultimate bowl series, often with skateparks built specifically for the event and then donated to the host city.

-**Red Bull Bowl Rippers.** Annual aerial combat at the historic Bowl Du Prado in fabulous Marseille.

-**Tampa Am/Pro.** The most democratic way to make a name for yourself in competitive skateboarding is in Tampa, where the industry giants have their eyes on you.

-**Vans Pool Party.** Takes place in the Vans Combi Pool in Orange County, California, and is the perfect place to find out who's who in concrete.

-**X Games.** The first televised action sports festival is considered "the Olympics of extreme sports" and continues to attract the biggest names in competitive skateboarding.

If you have enjoyed the skateboarding curiosities presented in this book, we would like to ask you to share a review on Amazon.

Your opinion is highly valuable to us and to other skate enthusiasts who are looking to be entertained and gain new knowledge about this sport.

We understand that leaving a comment can be a tedious process, but we kindly ask you to take a few minutes of your time to share your thoughts and opinions with us.

Your support is greatly important to us and helps us continue creating quality content for the fans of this incredible sport.

We appreciate your support and hope that you have enjoyed reading our book as much as we enjoyed writing it.

Thank you for sharing your experience with us!

★ ★ ★ ★ ★